God's
Fresh
Air

Living to Enjoy & Cherish a
Life of Purpose with God

Alicia M. Bailey

authorHOUSE®

AuthorHouse™
1663 Liberty Drive
Bloomington, IN 47403
www.authorhouse.com
Phone: 1 (800) 839-8640

Published by AuthorHouse   03/31/2016

ISBN: 978-1-5049-7512-4 (sc)
ISBN: 978-1-5049-7511-7 (e)

Acknowledgements and Dedications

This book is dedicated to my Lord and Savior Jesus Christ, who is the source of my life.

It is also dedicated to my husband, Marquis D. Bailey, who is the great love of my life. *"You have been a great source of support in my spiritual journey with God, the ministry that God has given me, and in writing this book. I appreciate all of your encouragement throughout this process. It has been much needed. Thanks so much and I love you!"*

I would like to thank and acknowledge my mother, Verdie Gore Morris, who has been one of my most faithful supporters.

I acknowledge my pastor, Pastor Michael Thomas, Senior Pastor of *"Love and Faith Christian Fellowship Church"*, who has been a spiritual mentor through his teachings and the word of God.

I acknowledge the *"Holiness Church of God"* and the church where I began my spiritual journey.

I would like to thank and acknowledge Minister John X. Miller of NBG Consulting for his guiding wisdom and support throughout the writing of this book.

I would also like to thank and acknowledge Michael Marshall of *Marshall Design Studio* for graphics and photography.

I acknowledge a host of family members and relatives who have supported me in the ministry that God has given to me.

This book has played a part in my spiritual journey. I have grown and learned a great deal through this process, and I count it all joy. I hope to encourage all women to live the life God intended you to live.

May God Bless you in every part of your life.

CONTENTS

Part 1: Inhaling the New You

Part 2: Exhaling Purpose

Part 3: Keep Breathing Freely

PREFACE

There she sat on the cramped closet floor weeping as tears ran down her cheeks.

"There has to be more to me than this," she thought. As she lifted her head, in a faint small voice she cried out "Lord who am I? Tell me who I am so that I can breathe your fresh air!"

And like the dew in the morning, He gently rested upon her heart.

That weeping woman was me many years ago. Like many women today, I needed to find out who I was so that I could breathe God's Fresh Air. I struggled with knowing my purpose and thinking to myself, "Why have I been placed on earth?" I had been given many talents and gifts from God, but what were they for? There had to be more for me than just going to work and coming home because I just simply existed, going through the motions of life. And I didn't want to simply exist anymore. Instead, I desired to do more with my life. I wanted to make my mark on earth and bring glory to God in every part of life.

In other words, I wanted to breathe God's Fresh Air. But how could I do that if I didn't know who I was or what I was called to do? Through the word of God, I found out who I really was and I began to live a more purpose-filled life which allowed me to finally breathe freely in the Lord. Many women today just like me yearn to fulfill their purpose in life and desire to breathe God's Fresh Air. Breathing freely in the Lord does not mean that you have reached perfection and that you no longer need God. But it simply means that you live every day to be the best person that you can be by striving to fulfill purpose daily. It means that God gets the glory from your life and that you cherish every moment of life by living a life of purpose in God.

God intends for each of us to live a healthy, purpose-filled lifestyle, spiritually and mentally, so that He gets the glory from it all. In other words, God desires for us to "live on purpose" so that we can breathe freely in Him every day.

In this book, I hope to inspire every woman to "live on purpose" by living the life that God intended for you to live. The motivation of this book has been inspired by my own spiritual experiences in life and most importantly, the word of God. I hope to encourage spiritual growth in God and confidence in all women, allowing you to inhale a new perspective of who you are and exhale the glory of God in your life. Writing this book was an inspiration to my heart, and I hope it blesses your life as it has mine.

For more information on this book and resources on the word of God please visit the website at www.aliciabaileyministries.com.

PART 1: INHALING THE NEW YOU

CHAPTER 1

WAKE-UP! THIS IS YOUR SPIRITUAL AWAKENING

Each morning as the day begins, millions of women are awaken by the sound of a ringing alarm clock. From the start of the day, you are full-speed ahead never stopping for a moment to breathe God's Fresh Air and cherish the moments of life. Husbands, children, extended family and co-workers along with decisions, meetings and phone calls are all awaiting your presence. Before you even dawn a new day, you are exhausted just thinking about the day ahead. In the midst of all of the day's demands, you are simply sleep walking through life.

Wake-up! This is your spiritual awakening!

Sleep walking is a sleep disorder in which the body is in motion yet the mind is dormant. Unfortunately, many women are sleep walking through life. They are in motion and completing the tasks at hand, however, their minds are elsewhere. But there is something more for you than just going through the motions of life. You were created for something greater and that something greater is to bring glory to God. I believe that God is saying "Breathe My Fresh Air."

Take a moment to look away from the hectic schedules of life to ponder the memory from where God has brought you and visualize where He will take you in this journey of life. Life is tough but God is tougher, and it is because of His grace and mercy that you have survived thus far.

During my journey in life, just like many women, I've had to come to the realization that everything I was, everything I am, and everything

I hope to become is because of God. I realized that my life was not about me at all but it is about bringing glory to God.

So I asked God the question, "How do I bring glory to you?" His answer was by cherishing every day and never taking a moment for granted. The truth is, we don't know the day or the hour when God will call us home and so we should live every day treasuring every moment. As a result, my goal was and is to be the best me I can be and live life to the fullest every day. In other words, I began to live life on purpose. From that moment on, I began to savor every moment by being grateful to God for my life, the people in it, and for what He has done. I discovered that by valuing the larger and smaller things in life, I somehow became happier and surprisingly healthier. I took the time to appreciate everything that God had done in my life and as a result I began to breathe freely. So today I encourage you to enjoy your children, love your husband, befriend your friends, love yourself and most importantly be grateful to God, so that He will get the glory from your life.

When you feel overwhelmed by the many responsibilities in life such as parenting, marriage, career, relationships, and even conflicts, remember that God is with you. So relax. He's God, and He has it all under control. You must learn to let God have His way so that you can embrace the sweet fragrance of God and breathe freely.

However, it can sometimes become challenging to find the time to breathe the fragrance of the Master's aroma, but in order to become what God designed you to be, you must stop and breathe. Take a moment to peer through the window of your life. You will find you have a lot to be thankful for.

As a child, my mother would sing a popular nursery rhyme in which a spider would climb up the water spout and suddenly the rain would wash the spider back down. After the rain, the sun would come out to dry the rain away and the spider would climb back up again to continue her chores. As I thought about the spider, this persistent creature that worked extremely hard even after a storm had washed her away, I realized that she was focused on her chores. She never took a moment to look at the beautiful sun that came to her rescue. That was her problem.

Ironically, many women are so devoted to the duties of life that even after a storm or a troublesome circumstance has occurred in their life and *the son, Jesus Christ,* comes to wipe away their pain they forget to be thankful.

It is only because of the son of God, Jesus, that we are capable of accomplishing the many demands that are expected of us each day and as a result, we owe God a moment of our time.

In the Bible, Martha worked so hard on her task that she forgot her purpose, which was to serve Jesus. But her sister, Mary, took a moment to worship in the presence of her Savior –*Luke 10:38-42.* Don't be another Martha. Instead be like Mary and take a moment to worship and cherish God. After all, He's our Father. He knows us by name, and He loves us dearly. So I am announcing your wake-up call is now. The concierge has dialed your hotel room number, and it is time to wake up.

Today is a day of new beginnings. *"Old things are passed away and behold all things shall become new"*--*2 Corinthians 5:17 (KJV).* Starting today you are a new creature in Christ. When you step out of bed shout, *"This is the day the Lord has made and I will rejoice and be glad in it."*— *Psalms 118:24 (NIV).*

Don't dread the day ahead. After all, this is another day that you are alive. God is kissing you good morning because you are purposed to bring Him glory. Tell the Lord you love Him and breathe in His goodness.

As you wake your child, embrace their beautiful faces and encourage them to be all that God has called for them to become. Love your husband and adorn him with an intimate kiss. Remember that you are a child of the Most High God, purposed to bring glory and honor to God's name. People should see God in you and His goodness in your home, on your job, in your relationships and in everything you do. And you should cherish every moment in life.

Now that's living for a purpose and breathing God's Fresh Air. So today, wake up to be refreshed and cherish every moment.

"This is your Spiritual Awakening!"

Chapter 1: Notes and Study Questions

Chapter Focus: *This chapter focuses on a spiritual awakening, encouraging you to breathe God's Fresh Air. Breathing God's Fresh Air means to take the time to enjoy and cherish life as God intends for every believer to do. Throughout the upcoming chapters you will gain spiritual principles on how to enjoy and cherish life with God (Breathe God's Fresh Air).*

Do you need a spiritual awakening? If so, Why?
How do you bring glory and honor to God in your life?

_____

_____

_____

_____

_____

_____

_____

_____

_____

_____

What do you want to gain from reading this book?

_____

_____

_____

_____

_____

_____

_____

_____

_____

_____

Did this chapter change your thinking? How?

_____

_____

_____

_____

_____

_____

_____

_____

_____

_____

_____

Chapter 2

Who are you in Christ?

There comes a time in life when every woman should reach a spiritual maturity in which they no longer allow people or material things to define who they are. Instead they look to God. Many women struggle to find who they are in Christ, because the world has used titles, roles, and even possessions to define who they are.

When asked the question who are you? Many people will give their job title or position. But the question is not who are you in the world? The question is who are you in Christ? Who you are is much deeper than worldly titles, possessions, and the opinions of others.

In my life, I had to realize that I was more than just an educator or school administrator. I was more than just a church member or a speaker. I was even more than just a sister, daughter, or wife. But I am a disciple of Christ.

Defining who you are in Christ requires you to look deeply into yourself and the word of God. It requires you to evaluate the bigger picture of identity. In other words, you must intensely evaluate yourself. This evaluation considers your behaviors, values, strengths and weaknesses, likes and dislikes. Self-evaluation is an essential part of finding who you are in Christ and it requires extreme honesty. Being honest with yourself helps you to discover who you are in the Lord.

So let's begin this spiritual journey of self-discovery.

"Who are you?"

Take a moment to make a self-discovery list of everything you know about yourself. Think deeply about who you really are. This list should not include superficial blessings such as material things but should represent your character, values, behaviors, likes and dislikes. Your self-discovery list should include your strengths and even your weaknesses. The purpose of this list is to help you along your spiritual journey of self-discovery. Look inside yourself to find that virtuous woman that God has created *--Proverbs 31:10-31.*

Ask yourself these questions.

"What are my strengths and what are my weaknesses?"

"What do I enjoy in life and what do I dislike?"

"What am I afraid of and what am I thankful or glad about?"

"How do I handle difficulty and how do I celebrate success?"

Do not share these answers with anyone. This self-discovery list is for your eyes only, so be honest. Your list can be as long or as detailed as you like. Ask yourself honestly "Who am I?"

By now, you may be wondering why this list is important. Well, this self-discovery list was essential for my own spiritual journey of breathing God's Fresh Air. And it will be essential to your spiritual journey as well.

One morning at about 3am, I was having difficulty falling asleep. I began to list everything I knew about myself. I drew a circle and wrote my name on the inside and on the outside of the circle I began to write things I knew about myself. I thought of as many details as I could. Some of the details listed were small such as "likes pizza" and some were big such as "hypertension." For three days, I worked on this list, writing down everything I knew about myself. Some details were embarrassing, some were humorous, but they were all about me. I had no idea why God had told me to make this list, yet I was intrigued and eager to complete it.

When I finished, I placed it under my mattress because it was personal and I did not want anyone to see it. For several days, I kept going back and forth to look at it. Why did God have me write it? What was it for? Finally, one night I picked it up and began to ponder the things that I had written and suddenly I realized that my list was unique. No one in this whole world could make a list exactly like mine.

None of it focused on material things such as a car, a house, or a bank account. But all of it had to do with who I was inside. At that moment, I realized that all 122 details I had written about myself were not so bad after all. In fact, my list was *good enough* and if it was good enough that meant I was good enough. After all, the list was about me, right? Yes, there were some things listed that I needed to improve on and things listed that I was not proud of, but it was still good enough.

Many women have been conditioned by life's circumstances, television and media to believe that they don't measure up. In fact, the world would have you believe that you are not good enough. Many women have convinced themselves that they have to become more than whom they really are, and they are pressured to live up to the standards of a superficial society. But you must understand that despite human flaws, shortcomings and mistakes you are still good enough for God. God can use us all, and He will never cast you aside or turn you away--*John 6:37.* In other words, you are good enough for God to use.

As you ponder your self-discovery list, you should realize that your list is matchless. Indeed, *you are the salt of the earth--Matthew 5:13 (NIV)* and you are created uniquely. God said, *"I knew you before you were formed in your mother's womb and before you were born I set you apart"--Jeremiah 1:5 (NLT).*

Everyone has made mistakes and has regrets. We all have strengths, weaknesses and areas to grow but we are still good enough for God to use. You should not compare yourself to other people or measure yourself by material gain.

Instead you should look to God because He is our source and provider. Never make excuses for who you are based upon what the media or television say women should be or look like. Instead, you should be proud of whom you are in Christ and rely only on what the word of God teaches. As a believer, you have been charged to be the best you that you can be. Today I ask you, "Who are you in Christ?" The answer: You are a unique woman of God that is good enough for God to use in extraordinary ways!

Chapter 2: Notes and Study Questions

Chapter Focus: *This chapter focuses on finding who you are in Christ. In this chapter you will conduct a self-evaluation and a study of who you really are in Christ. The lesson learned from this chapter is that every woman is unique and God loves us all despite our unique differences. You are good enough for God to use in extraordinary ways.*

Who are you in Christ?

(Name)_____

Strengths: _____   Weaknesses: _____

_____   _____

_____   _____

_____   _____

Likes: _____   Dislikes: _____

_____   _____

_____   _____

_____   _____

What am I good at?_____   What's unique about me?_____

_____   _____

_____   _____

_____   _____

_____   _____

What are my God-given gifts?____   _____

_____   _____

_____   _____

_____   _____

_____   _____

<u>Alternative: Who are you in Christ?</u>

Use either list. This page or the previous page will benefit you. Add as many circles as needed.

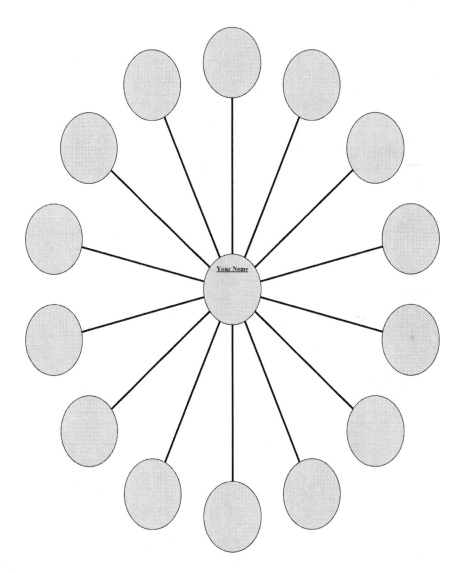

Chapter 2: Notes and Study Questions

How has this chapter affected you spiritually?

_____

_____

_____

_____

_____

_____

_____

_____

_____

_____

Notes:

_____

_____

_____

_____

_____

_____

_____

_____

_____

_____

_____

_____

_____

_____

_____

_____

_____

CHAPTER 3

RELINQUISH CONTROL AND TRUST GOD

One of the main reasons many women cannot breathe freely in the Lord is because they have not relinquished control to God. Are you a person who attempts to dictate how everything around you is done? Are you a person who has to be in control of everything? Are you easily frustrated when others around you are not behaving as you want them too? Do you become stressed when you do not know what is going to happen in the future? If you answered "yes" to any of these questions then you may need to relinquish control to God. I say that because I was a person who needed to relinquish control to the Lord.

At one point in my life I wanted to control everything in life. I was a planner and I wanted to plan and organize everything. I wanted to know what was going to happen, how it was going to happen, and when it was going to happen. I wanted to know all the details about life and I tried to plan everything out. The truth is I wanted to control everything. When in fact, I was not controlling anything.

In my experience, trying to control life without the Lord is exhausting because when things do not go according to plan you became stressed and frustrated. As a result, you use up your own energy trying to handle things on your own. Through my own life experiences and relationship with God I realized that I could not control everything in life. And as I grew and matured into the woman I am today I had to face the harsh reality that there are things in life that are beyond my control. In fact, I had to relinquish control to the Lord.

The bottom line is you cannot control other people's feelings, thoughts, behaviors, or attitudes. You cannot control the decisions or choices that other adults or family members make. You cannot control the actions of members in the congregation or co-workers on your job. You can *only* control the things that God has entrusted to you. As for the other things in life that are beyond your control, you must let go and let God have His way. In other words, you must relinquish control to the Lord if you really want to breathe freely in God.

Relinquishing control to the Lord requires you to trust Him with your life. Trust is defined as the belief that someone is reliable, good, and honest. To trust someone means that you believe that they have your best interest at heart and no one is as trustworthy as God. The truth is you can trust God with your life because He loves you. God's love is so deep that He can be trusted with every problem or concern that occurs in your life. He can be trusted to wipe away the sin of your past and implement the promises of your future. God will never let you down, never give up on you, and never leave you alone because He loves you. This is why the Bible teaches us to, *"Cast all of your cares or worries to God because He cares for us."—1 Peter 5:7 (NLT)*. In other words, you can trust in the Lord because He loves you. Therefore, you don't have to try to control life on your own but instead you can *"Trust in the LORD with all your heart and lean not on your own understanding;" –Proverbs 3:5 (NIV)*.

When you try to control things yourself, you say to the Lord that His power is not good enough or strong enough to handle your situation. When you try to control things on your own, you run the risk of blocking your blessings and getting in the way of God's promises. But instead, you must learn to rest in the finished works of the Lord Jesus Christ because He has already made provisions for your problem to be solved. In fact, He's got it all under control. Relinquishing control and trusting God means that you surrender all of your problems and concerns to the Lord by believing in Him.

In life, there are things that you cannot control with your own human strength but the Lord Jesus Christ can. Jesus said, *"With man this is impossible, but with God all things are possible." – Matthew 19:26 (KJV)*.

By relinquishing control and trusting God you can walk in *"the peace of God, which passeth all understanding"—Philippians 4:7(KJV)*. There is a sweet peace of mind that you gain when you put your trust in the Lord and relinquish control to Him. After all, you're not controlling life anyway. God should be in control of your life.

I encourage you to allow yourself to be guided through life by trusting in the Lord Jesus Christ and be confident that God can take care of everything in your life. In fact, He has everything under control. So as your life dawns a new day of breathing God's Fresh Air, do your best to relinquish control and trust God to work on your behalf.

Chapter 3: Notes and Study Questions

Chapter Focus: *This chapter focuses on the importance of trusting God to control your life. In order to relinquish control of your life to God, you must put your trust in Him. Relinquishing control of your life by putting your trust in God is a key principle that will allow you to enjoy and cherish life (Breathe God's Fresh Air).*

Have you tried to control a situation that was beyond your control? If so, what was it?

_____

_____

_____

_____

_____

_____

_____

_____

_____

_____

Do you need to relinquish control of your life to God? In what area?

_____

_____

_____

_____

_____

_____

_____

_____

_____

_____

_____

Notes:

_____

_____

_____

_____

_____

_____

_____

_____

_____

_____

_____

_____

_____

_____

_____

_____

_____

_____

CHAPTER 4

BALANCE YOUR LIFE

After a long day of work, have you ever asked yourself, "What have I actually accomplished? Have I made a difference today?" only to realize that you had worked all day completing a hodgepodge of tasks that really did not matter in the real scheme of life? I have and that's when I came to the realization that I needed balance in my life.

I was exhausted, overworked, and overwhelmed with a countless number of tasks that seemed like busy work in the big picture of life.

I did not feel as if I was accomplishing my purpose in life. Instead, I felt unfulfilled as if I was simply completing task after task. I was mentally and physically drained because I was neglecting what I enjoyed most and as a result it affected my health. For me, balance had to become a priority. After all, how could I be effective as a member of the body of Christ when I was not being effective in my own life? --1 Timothy 3:5.

I needed to focus on the important things in life. I did not want to neglect my daily responsibilities of everyday assignments such as my job or career, but I needed to set boundaries for myself because I was being consumed with a countless number of tasks. In other words, I needed to find balance in my life so that I could breathe freely and the only way to find balance was to prioritize my time.

I had to decide what was most important in my life and make it a priority. At that moment, my new priorities became my health, time with my family, and most importantly, time with God became sacred. By taking the time to prioritize my life through the power of the Holy Spirit, I began to live a more balanced life which allowed me to breathe freely and live healthier and happier.

Take a moment to examine your life. Are you pleased with how you spend your time? If not, you may need to prioritize your time to create balance in your life.

Prioritizing to create balance in your life will require you to figure out what's most important to you. Is it your career, family, or even your preferred hobby? For some this may be an easy decision to make but for others it may be difficult to decide. If you are not able to immediately and honestly make a decision on what is most important to you, then it may help to step away for a few days all by yourself to make your decision easier.

During your time away, you should reflect on the thing you miss the most. The thing that you miss the most is what is important to you. In fact, the three most important things to you should be your top priorities in life. Out of the three, one of those top priorities should be time with God.

The Bible teaches to *seek first the kingdom of God and His righteousness --Matthew 6:33 (NIV)*. If you *seek His will in all you do then He will show you which path to take --Proverbs 3:6 (NLT)*. This means that your first priority should be your relationship with God so that He can guide your path.

Once you have identified what is most important to you, your overall goals and purpose for each day should reflect your top priorities. Take the time to establish a set amount of time to focus on your top three priorities each day. In my life, I had to create time each day for prayer and meditation, exercise, and time with my husband. I did not neglect my daily duties or become irresponsible, but time for these top priorities became sacred.

In fact, I became a protector of my priorities. During this protected time, I turned off my cell phone, email, and eliminated any other distractions because I needed balance in my life so that I could breathe freely in the Lord. And honestly, it was a challenge because I had to learn to say *"no"* to certain tasks in order to keep my top priorities. Saying *"no"* is difficult for many women because we often desire to please others. We often desire to do everything and be there for everyone. But the Bible teaches us to live life to please God because *if you are trying to please man, then you will not be a servant of Christ --Galatians 1:10 (ESV).* Therefore, become a protector of your priorities so that you can find balance in your life.

Finding balance in life takes hard work and understanding that you cannot accomplish everything in one day. Some things and some people will have to wait until tomorrow. I encourage you to develop a time management plan.

Beyond your top priorities, focus your time and daily tasks on what you can do today. It's easy to become overwhelmed by looking at the big picture. As a result, you try to complete too many tasks in one day causing you not to put forth your best efforts. Live for today by establishing a set time for your three top priorities. Then decide what other tasks can be accomplished within the day, and the rest should go on your to-do-list for the next day. Now that's finding balance!

Finding balance in life gives you a sense of peace, allows you to focus on the important things, and lends time for you to enjoy life. Imbalance creates stress, anxiety, and insomnia which results in neglect and exhaustion. But when your life is balanced, you can feel and see the results of a healthier life. Find the time to balance your life so that you can breathe freely in the Lord and begin seeing the results in life.

Chapter 4: Notes and Study Questions

Chapter Focus: *This chapter focuses on finding balance in your life and encourages you to evaluate how you spend your time. In this chapter, you gain strategies to prioritize life and you are encouraged to spend time focusing on the important things in life which will allow you to enjoy and cherish life more (Breathe God's Fresh Air).*

What is most important to you?

_____

_____

_____

_____

_____

_____

_____

_____

_____

What are your top three priorities?

_____

_____

_____

_____

_____

_____

_____

_____

_____

What time will you set to focus on each of your top priorities?

Example: _Create your own schedule_	
1.) Daily Prayer and Meditation 2.) Date Night with Spouse 3.) Daily Exercise Jog/Walk	1.) Early morning from 5am-5:45am 2.) Every Thursday Night 3.) Every afternoon from 4:15pm-5pm
1.)	
2.)	
3.)	

Notes:

_____

_____

_____

_____

_____

_____

_____

_____

_____

_____

_____

_____

_____

_____

_____

_____

Part 2: Exhaling Purpose

CHAPTER 5

DISCOVERING AND FULFILLING PURPOSE

Purpose is defined as the reason for which something is created or for which something exists. There are two types of purpose for our lives. There is a "shared purpose" which is the general mission that every believer in the body of Christ is assigned to carry out. And there is an "individual purpose" that is the unique calling or passion that is assigned solely to you.

All Christian believers have a shared purpose to spread the love of Christ through the power of the Holy Spirit and bring glory to God. This does not mean that every believer is to become a preacher or pastor, but every believer is purposed to represent Christ in their home, on their job, and in the world. The lifestyle that you live everyday should direct others closer to God. This means that you are purposed to be a witness of the good news of Jesus Christ by the way you live your everyday life. People around you should see the power of the Holy Spirit working within you by the way you treat others and the way you handle your day-to-day activities. The believer should be an example of Christ for the lost and unbelieving. In other words, you are charged with a shared purpose to spread the love of Christ to a dying world and bring glory to God. This shared purpose for the believer is our general mission for living. It is the heart that beats in the body of Christ and you should strive to fulfill this shared purpose every day of your life.

In addition to having a shared purpose, God assigns each of us an individual purpose to fulfill. Discovering and fulfilling that individual purpose comes from the power of the Holy Spirit within you.

Our individual purpose is the calling or passion that lies within each of us, the drive that pushes us to do more and be more. It is the unique gift given to us that comes with ease. Through our personal life experiences, God molds and shapes each of us to fulfill our individual purpose. In other words, your individual purpose is unique to only you. From the moment you are formed in the womb, He prepares you to fulfill your purpose. However, it is important to know that people discover and fulfill their calling or individual purpose at different times; some early in life and some later. Nevertheless, it is in God's perfect timing—*Ecclesiastes 3:1, Habakkuk 2:3.*

You cannot predict when doors will open but you can simply trust and pray that they will open. The word of God teaches *"The Lord will withhold no good thing from those who do what is right"—Psalms 84:11 (NLT).* So we trust that God wants us to succeed and do well. He wants each of us to discover and fulfill our calling or individual purpose. And He reveals that purpose to us at His appointed time—*Ecclesiastes 3:1.*

The secret to discovering or fulfilling your calling or individual purpose is not in a 10-step guide book or a purpose-driven class or conference, but the secret to discovering and fulfilling your purpose is by taking hold to God's never-changing hand and asking the Holy Spirit to reveal what He wants to do in your life.

And once you have discovered your calling or individual purpose, you are charged to be a good steward over it and fulfill it to the best of your ability so that you bring glory to God. Bringing glory to God through your individual purpose helps you to fulfill your shared purpose.

Pray for God to reveal your calling or individual purpose and once He has done that, study it, grow it, and perfect it so that you can fulfill it. Keep in mind that purpose is not always glitzy or glamorous. It is not always fame and fireworks. In fact, fulfilling your purpose is hard work. It takes dedication, patience, and an incredible amount of endurance.

Jesus had the ultimate purpose, and it was neither glitz nor glamour. Indeed, it was a true test of character and Jesus had great character. So as a believer you should pray to discover and fulfill your purpose as Jesus fulfilled His purpose. Despite of challenging circumstances or trials, you are created to discover and fulfill your purpose in life—*Romans 8:28.*

Through prayer and meditation, God will reveal His purpose for your life and He will also provide the provisions and resources you need to fulfill it. So I encourage you to stand on the promises of God, spread the love of Christ, and bring glory to His name so that you will fulfill the purpose on your life.

Chapter 5: Notes and Study Questions

Chapter Focus: *This chapter focuses on discovering your shared purpose and individual purpose. Our shared purpose is to spread the love of Christ and bring glory to God. Your calling or individual purpose is unique to only you. In this chapter, you are encouraged to fulfill the shared purpose of every believer and pray to God for the revelation of His individual purpose for your life. When you live life on purpose, you can breathe freely in the Lord.*

What kind of example do you set for others (in your home, job, in the world)? Can others see Christ in your life? If not, why?

_____

_____

_____

_____

_____

_____

_____

_____

What gift do you possess? How do you know?

_____

_____

_____

_____

_____

_____

_____

_____

How do you plan to develop, grow, and use this gift or calling?

_____

_____

_____

_____

_____

_____

_____

_____

_____

What do you believe your calling or individual purpose is and how will it bring glory to God?

_____

_____

_____

_____

_____

_____

_____

_____

_____

Chapter 6

Embrace the Unfamiliar

Embracing the unfamiliar means to be open minded to what God wants to do in your life.

After God revealed His individual purpose for my life, I was eager to fulfill it and I was on a mission for God. I was ready to accept the task that He wanted me to accomplish, as long as it was comfortable. For years, I had attended the same church. In fact, I grew up there. My family was there, and it was comfortable. I began my journey singing in the choir as a small child and later I became the choir director.

From there, God called me to minister His word and I became the youth minister of the church. Soon after, God continued to work in my life and I became an associate minister of the ministry and women's ministry coordinator. I was comfortable there. I respected my pastor and I loved the ministry. As a result, I was dedicated and I enjoyed what God had called me to do.

However, one night I was reading God's word and studying for an upcoming sermon, and I realized that for months I had been preaching from the same scriptures. My focus was on the book of Genesis and the biblical character of Abram. I was captivated by Abram's life and what he endured in order to reach his destiny.

From the beginning, Abram was destined for greatness but in order for him to fulfill this great destiny God had to remove Abram from his comfort zone. Here was a man that God had purposed for something great yet he could not fulfill the call while he was still living in the familiar territory of his homeland--*Genesis 12:1*. It was not until after Abram left his comfort zone that his purpose was fulfilled.

The Bible teaches that the Lord instructed Abram to leave his homeland and travel to a Promised Land. And as a result of his obedience, the Lord made a covenant promise to Abram, to bless and make his name great as well as to make him a father of many nations. In order for Abram to possess all of the great things that he had been promised, he had to be open minded to accept the challenge of embracing the unfamiliar. God had to remove Abram from the familiar territory of his homeland and place him in an unfamiliar situation so that he could grow and fulfill the purpose on his life.

In other words, there may be times in life when God will take you out of your comfort zone. Stepping out of your comfort zone makes you dependent upon the Lord and trying new things opens a world of new possibilities and opportunities.

After studying the scriptures, God revealed to me why He had me focus and minister from this lesson. My time in my comfort zone had come to an end. God was challenging me to leave my former church and embrace a new beginning in a new ministry. And honestly, it was difficult to embrace the challenge because it was uncomfortable and unfamiliar territory. I loved the people in that ministry; some of them were even family members but God had a different plan for my life. I have to admit I was slow to move because in the natural realm I wanted to stay, but in the spiritual realm I had to go. I prayed, fasted, and even hoped that God would change His mind. But He did not because I have to fulfill the purpose in my life.

That year I stepped down as associate minister and left the ministry to embrace the unfamiliar territory of a new church and ministry. Once I embraced my new unfamiliar territory, God began to open doors and provide spiritual opportunities that I never thought possible. I began to learn and grow in different aspects of the word and in ministry. I still appreciated and respected where God had brought me from but I also embraced where God was taking me.

Embracing the unfamiliar takes obedience, courage, and sometimes it takes discomfort. It is important that you understand that I am *not* advising you leave your church. But I am simply using my own experience as an example of stepping out of my comfort zone to fulfill my purpose. Perhaps God is commissioning you to embrace a new career, challenging you to sharpen a skill or hobby, urging you to reach out to someone in need, or soliciting you to do something you've never done before. I encourage you to step out of your comfort zone and embrace the unfamiliar.

It is essential to know that when you step out of your comfort zone, you must be led by God. Sometimes God will use an unfamiliar situation to shape you into the person that you are called to be. When you step out of your comfort zone, you become totally dependent upon Him by putting your trust in God. We all should be willing to try new things in God so that we can fulfill the purpose on our lives.

Once Abram embraced the challenge of stepping out of his comfort zone, he experienced new things and became a new person. In fact, as a result of Abram's decision to obey God, his life was transformed and God changed his name from Abram to Abraham which means "Father of many nations." Abraham embraced the uncomfortable opportunities of life that were set before him by God.

This unfamiliar experience prepared and molded Abraham so that he could handle and fulfill the greatness on his life. I challenge you to step out of your comfort zone and embrace your unfamiliar territory, according to the will of God--*1 Peter 4:19,* so that you can breathe freely.

Chapter 6: Notes and Study Questions

Chapter Focus: *In this chapter you are encouraged to step out of your comfort zone so that purpose can be fulfilled in your life. Stepping out of your comfort zone requires you to listen to the voice of God. The chapter encourages you to put your trust in the Lord as you explore new things. Putting your trust in God allows you to enjoy and cherish life (Breathe God's Fresh Air).*

Is God commissioning you to step out of your comfort zone? If so, how do you know?

_____

_____

_____

_____

_____

_____

_____

_____

_____

_____

Will you trust God in unfamiliar territory? How?

_____

_____

_____

_____

_____

_____

_____

_____

_____

_____

Notes:

_____

_____

_____

_____

_____

_____

_____

_____

_____

_____

_____

_____

_____

_____

_____

_____

Chapter 7

Equipped for the Challenge

Every believer will encounter obstacles and challenges in life, even those that know who they are, cherish every moment, pray and meditate, fulfill purpose, and embrace new things. No matter how long you've been saved or how long you've had a relationship with Christ, it is inevitable that challenges will come. In fact, your relationship with Christ does not exempt you from challenges. But instead your relationship with Christ equips you to stand through these challenging times.

In my own experience, I remember when I first accepted Christ into my life. I thought I would not have to endure anymore negative situations, tests or trials, and that everything would be rosy and sweet. However, I found out very quickly that I was sadly mistaken. Even though I had developed a relationship with Christ, challenging situations still arose in life.

Even Jesus was tested in the wilderness and persecuted throughout biblical history. And if Jesus had to endure challenges then we will also. But we should take comfort that God has equipped us to stand through any test or trial. The bottom line is that life's challenges of misunderstandings, disappointments, and human shortcomings happen to everyone but we are equipped to make it through these challenges.

As a believer, you should view your challenges through the eyes of a different lens than the world. Every challenge you endure should be a learning experience so that you don't just go through the challenge but you grow through the challenge. In fact, many of the challenges you encounter in life will mold and shape you for greater purpose. Obstacles come to prepare you for your destiny, and tests come to make you and not break you. The believer is equipped to make it through any challenge or test in life.

But the question is "How?" How can we make it through challenging times? The answer: God has given every believer the gift of the Holy Spirit which helps you overcome any obstacle or challenge that may interrupt your life.

The Holy Spirit is the power of God at work in us. This Holy Spirit leads, guides, and gives you wisdom to handle life's situations. This means that you do not have to conquer or solve your problems alone. It is the Holy Spirit inside of you that triumphs over trials. This is why the Bible teaches, *"Ye are of God, little children, and have overcome: because greater is He that is in you, than he that is in the world." –1 John 4:4 (KJV).*

Therefore, you should take comfort that you do not have to endure alone. In other words, the greater power of the Holy Spirit that lives inside of you will give you the wisdom, knowledge, and provisions you need to handle any trial or challenge.

This Holy Spirit is what separates the believer from the unbeliever. Only the believer has a helper on the inside that orders their steps, gives guiding wisdom, and makes provisions on their behalf. Jesus teaches, *"But the Helper, the Holy Spirit, whom the Father will send in my name, He will teach you all things and bring to your remembrance all that I have said to you."—John 14:26 (NKJV).* This scripture ensures us that even though we all encounter challenges in life, the greater one inside of us has equipped each of us to stand.

It is important to remember that God is in control of your life and when obstacles come your way, you must activate your faith by agreeing with the Holy Spirit. When you agree with the Holy Spirit who lives inside of you, you cast out what the enemy has to say and the word of God begins to work on your behalf.

I thank God for the Holy Spirit in my life because through the power of the Holy Spirit, God has given me victory over trials. This is why the Bible teaches, *"No, despite all these things, overwhelming victory is ours through Christ, who loved us."—Romans 8:37 (NLT).* Therefore, take comfort in knowing that God has equipped you to withstand and overcome any challenge that comes your way so you can breathe God's Fresh Air freely.

Chapter 7: Notes and Study Questions

Chapter Focus: *This chapter focuses on the Holy Spirit that lives inside of every believer. The chapter emphasizes how the power of the Holy Spirit equips the believer to withstand any challenge that comes your way. When you depend on the power of the Holy Spirit, you can enjoy and cherish life more (Breathe God's Fresh Air).*

What did you gain from this chapter?

_____

_____

_____

_____

_____

_____

_____

_____

_____

_____

Find five scriptures about the Holy Spirit that will encourage your faith and write them here. Meditate on these scriptures when you need guidance or during challenging times.

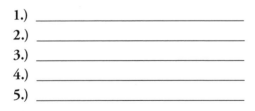

1.) _____

2.) _____

3.) _____

4.) _____

5.) _____

Notes:

_____

_____

_____

_____

Alicia M. Bailey

_____

_____

_____

_____

_____

_____

_____

_____

_____

_____

_____

_____

_____

_____

PART 3: KEEP BREATHING FREELY

CHAPTER 8

GOD'S GREAT GRACE

God's Great Grace is an on-going theme throughout the Bible. The word "Grace" comes from the Greek word *charis*, which means "kindness." Everyone should extend human grace or kindness to one another, but when the word grace is used in connection with God our Father, it takes on a much more powerful meaning.

God's Great Grace is the power of the Holy Spirit that is presented to the believer free of charge, enabling us to do what we could never do alone or with our own human strength. It is an undeserved gift of favor and kindness given by God. Grace is God choosing to bless His people rather than curse us as our sin deserves. In other words, it is His compassion on the undeserving human race and is given to us free of charge because He loves us.

Many people are misled to believe that you must earn God's kindness and love. Some believe that if you become good enough then you can work your way to God. In fact, I was one of those people. At one point in my life, living under Grace was a struggle because through religion and church traditions I had been taught that if I attended every church service, paid the right amount of money, and behaved just the right way then God would love and bless me. But for the Christian believer, this free gift of Grace is offered through faith in Jesus Christ, not by our own works or by our own human efforts but simply by believing and accepting God's love in our lives. This is why *Ephesians 2:8 (ESV)* teaches that *"For by grace are you saved, through faith, and this is not from your own doing."* In other words, you don't have to earn God's Grace; it is simply given to you through faith in Jesus Christ. All you have to do is believe.

This gift of Grace that is given through faith is sufficient enough to cover any amount of sin, failures, or problems--*2 Corinthians 12:9.* Therefore, you do not have to live a life of perfection but rather live a life of faith. It's not about being perfect through routines and traditions but about being faithful because if you love God you will live to please Him. He knows that the human race is not perfect and even after we confess our sin we will fall short again in some way, which is why Grace is given to us through faith.

But the challenge for many is to accept and live in this Grace. The truth is, many struggle to live under Grace because they have not fully accepted it in their lives. As a result, they live a life of commendation and struggle to breathe freely in the Lord.

But the solution to this problem is Jesus Christ, our Savior who was sent to shed His cleansing blood for the sin of mankind so that we can confidently live free of sin, guilt, and regret if we accept Him. By accepting Jesus into your life through faith, His loving kindness forgives, erases, and allows you to overcome in life.

However, you must understand that God's Grace does not give you permission to sin but it gives you the authority to break free from sin so that you are not held captive by it. The truth is, the enemy wants you to be held hostage by condemnation, past failures or even the mistakes you may make today. But God's Great Grace can cover a multitude of sin, for *where sin abounded, grace abounded much more. --Romans 5:20 (KJV).*

When you feel defeated or overwhelmed by your past, you should just simply begin to thank God for His Grace. Only God's Grace can wipe away your flaws and restore your confidence. It is only Grace that can change you into what God desires for you to become, but you must accept this Grace in your heart and learn to live in it. It is important to understand that the key to living in Grace is faith, not faith in your own abilities but faith in Jesus because He has enough Grace to meet and supply all of your needs.

I am so grateful for God's Great Grace in my life. For it was Grace that carried me through tough situations in life, Grace that brought me out of things I did not understand, and it is only by Grace that God will keep me in every part of life.

Receive and accept God's Great Grace in your life by asking Him for it. You should not live a life of defeat but you should live a victorious life under the Grace of God through faith. You should not beat yourself up with guilt, shame, or condemnation. Instead, depend on God's Grace to remove sin and restore your heart because you are God's heir under Grace. You are the righteousness of God through faith in Jesus Christ and you can be confident that sin does not have dominion over you.

I challenge you to let go of your past failures and mistakes to live a life where God's grace flourishes in you. Because without Grace, we all toil with life and everything becomes difficult or unusually challenging. But with God's Grace we breathe God's Fresh Air "*not by our might or power but by His Spirit*"--*Zechariah 4:6 (NIV)*. So starting today and everyday forward, accept God's Great Grace and allow Him to work in your life so that you can breathe God's Fresh Air freely.

Chapter 8: Notes and Study Questions

Chapter Focus: *This chapter focuses on God's Great Grace. God's Great Grace is given to the believer free of charge, enabling you to do what you could never do with your own human strength. The key to God's Great Grace working in your life is to receive and accept this Grace from God.*

Have you accepted God's Great Grace in your life?

_____

_____

_____

_____

_____

_____

_____

_____

_____

_____

Have you forgiven yourself for past mistakes or sin?
What do you need to forgive yourself for?

_____

_____

_____

_____

_____

_____

_____

_____

_____

_____

_____

_____

PRAYER AND MEDITATION

Breathing God's Fresh Air requires prayer and meditation for every part of your life. Prayer is the intimate connection between the Christian believer and God. Meditation is the thought-provoking study of His word. Prayer and meditation connects us spiritually with our Heavenly Father. It is the best way to communicate with Him. This daily communication of prayer and meditation is vital to having a relationship with God and breathing freely in the Lord.

On a personal note, prayer and meditation changed my life and has become an essential part of my spiritual walk with Christ. Both prayer and meditation are essential in every believer's spiritual life.

But the question is "Why?" Why is prayer and meditation so important for your spiritual journey? The answer: Prayer provides a platform for you to share your life with God. It offers an opportunity for you to confess your sin and ask for help in overcoming sin. Prayer is an act of praise, worship, and obedience which gives you the opportunity to express thanksgiving for the things He provides for you in life. In fact, prayer gives you a way to acknowledge that God is in control of your life. *1 Thessalonians 5:16-18 (NIV)* teaches the believer to *rejoice always, pray continually, give thanks in all circumstances for this is God's will for you in Christ.* In other words, you should pray every day about everything you do because prayer is essential for every believer to breathe freely in the Lord.

Even Jesus prayed to God and that lets the believer know that we should pray also. As a daughter of Christ, you should strive to form a strong bonding relationship with your Heavenly Father through prayer and meditation. However, I advise you that strong relationships require time and commitment. For example, a woman's relationship with her husband will never become strong if she does not spend enough time with him. The same goes for your relationship with God. If you never spend time with God in prayer and meditation then your spiritual relationship with the Lord will not grow or become strong. And every believer needs a strong spiritual relationship with God through prayer so that He can guide our lives.

The truth is, we need prayer because life without communication with God is complicated. Many times in my life I have tried to handle things on my own without seeking the Lord through prayer, only to realize that I was using up my own energy trying to do what only God could do. Neglecting prayer and meditation with God makes you dependent on your own human wisdom to handle your situations. And in my experience, the more I try to handle things on my own without the Lord, the more complicated life becomes.

When you move ahead with a project, take a new position or job, or even begin a new relationship without seeking the Lord's guidance through prayer and meditation, it is subject to failure. Seeking guidance through prayer and meditation gives us all the wisdom we need to handle things better, communicate more effectively and stay in line with the plans of the Lord Jesus Christ. As a result, you can breathe freely in the Lord.

Another question is, "How should we pray?" Many people struggle with how to pray, with the right words to say in prayer, and how to communicate with God. Prayer is simple. Jesus gave His disciples the Lord's Prayer as an example of how to pray. You have the choice to recite the Lord's Prayer with its exact words or you can use your own words, by remembering the different parts of the prayer that Jesus wants us to include. The Lord's Prayer reads as follows:

*Our Father who art in heaven, hallowed be thy name. Thy kingdom come. Thy will be done on earth as it is in heaven. (**Humbleness**)*
Give us this day our daily bread, and forgive
*us our trespasses (**Repentance**),*
*as we forgive those who trespass against us (**Forgiviness**),*
*and lead us not into temptation, but deliver us from evil (**Righteousness**).*

For thine is the kingdom, and the power, and
*the glory, for ever and ever (**Honor**).*
Amen.
--Matthew 6:9-13 (KJV)

By following the example of the Lord's Prayer in your own words, you'll learn to honor God in your prayers. The Lord's Prayer reminds the believer that when you pray you should make yourself humble and forgiving. You should repent and honor God for all He has done. Remember that a forgiving man who asks God's forgiveness is forgiven, a generous man who seeks blessings from God will be blessed, and a merciful man who seeks God's mercy will be given God's mercy. Therefore, when you pray, you must forgive others, humble yourself, and repent from sin. This is why the Bible teaches, *"If my people, who are called by my name, will humble themselves and pray and seek my face and turn from their wicked ways, then will I hear from heaven and will forgive their sin and will heal their land."-- 2 Chronicles 7:14 (NIV)*

It is never difficult to communicate with God. When you speak to God, your speech does not need to be complicated or eloquent. Just a simple "God I need you (humbleness) and God have mercy or God forgive me (repentance)" will suffice. Oftentimes in prayer, we want to say exactly the right things but God is not looking for perfection. He is looking for humility. Don't get caught up in fancy wording just simply talk to God and He will hear you. You can be confident that He knows everything about you and everything you need. Even when we don't know what to say in prayer the Holy Spirit knows what we need. The Bible teaches, *"In the same way, the Spirit helps us in our weakness. We do not know what we ought to pray for, but the Spirit Himself intercedes for us through wordless groans."-- Romans 8:26 (NIV)*

While in prayer, it is important to be confident that God knows about every situation that you encounter in life. In fact, He gives us scripture to help us through every situation. When you are in prayer for a specific situation in life, you can ask God for what you need then meditate on a scriptural reference. This helps you stay focused on the promises of God and in agreement with His word. The Bible teaches us to *"Study this Book of Instruction continually. Meditate on it day and night so you will be sure to obey everything written in it. Only then will you prosper and succeed in all you do."-- Joshua 1:8 (NLT)*

This week set a goal to spend more time strengthening your relationship with the Lord through prayer and meditation. Escape into a private place so your conversation with the Lord will not be disturbed. Turn off your cell phone. Minimize other distractions because your time in prayer and meditation with the Lord is sacred.

Keep in mind that your conversation with God does not have to be complicated or politically correct. This conversation with the Lord can be as detailed and intimate as you desire. After all, He knows everything about you. You are His daughter, an heir to His throne and He loves you. I challenge and encourage you to wake up a little earlier, go to bed just a little later, or take time out of your busy schedule to communicate with God through prayer and meditation so that you can breathe freely in the Lord.

Chapter 9: Notes and Study Questions

Chapter Focus: *This chapter focuses on the importance of prayer and meditation in your daily walk with Christ. In this chapter you gain strategies on how to pray and meditate. It emphasizes that prayer and meditation are key principles to enjoying and cherishing life (Breathing God's Fresh Air).*

Take a moment to set up prayer and meditation time.

When will you take time to pray and meditate? (Example: 15 minutes during the morning, before dinner, after my workout, etc...)

_____

_____

_____

Where will you have your prayer and meditation? (Choose a place where you will not be disturbed.)

_____

_____

_____

_____

_____

How will you ensure that your time with God is not disturbed? (Phone calls, children, family, pets, etc...)

_____

_____

_____

_____

_____

_____

_____

What do you hope to gain from your time with God?

_____

_____

_____

_____

_____

_____

_____

_____

_____

_____

How will you pray?

_____

_____

_____

_____

CHAPTER **10**

LIVE WITH A GRATEFUL HEART

Living your life with a grateful heart makes breathing freely in the Lord a lot easier. A grateful heart and thanksgiving to God for all His blessings should be one of the most distinctive marks of the Christian believer in Jesus Christ. To be grateful is a feeling or showing of appreciation for God's kindness. To be grateful means to be thankful to God. The believer should be grateful for everything.

For many people gratefulness only comes during the Holiday Season or during Thanksgiving. But for the believer, gratefulness is a way of life. We should be grateful every day for everything. From the smallest detail to largest blessing we should have a grateful heart. The Bible teaches, *"In everything give thanks: for this is the will of God in Christ Jesus concerning you."*-- *1 Thessalonians 5:18* (KJV). God wants us to be thankful for everything.

I remember many years ago, my husband and I were in the grocery store at the deli counter. We were completing our normal weekend chore of grocery shopping. As we stood in line, I began to feel a sense of thanksgiving and gratefulness for simply the opportunity to shop. The longer we stood at the counter the more grateful I became. Suddenly, I found myself overjoyed with gratefulness and tears of thanksgiving ran down my face. As you can imagine, for my husband this was a little unexpected and embarrassing because we were simply ordering deli meat.

However, in my eyes, on that day, it was much more. In fact, it was a victory that deserved a victory dance because as a child I recall not having the luxury of eating fresh deli meat. In fact, I recall in eating *"Spam"* and

Bologna which are popular canned and processed meats. At that moment, I realized that God had taken me from "processed meat to the fresh deli counter." In other words, God had transitioned me from one realm into the next realm, so I was overjoyed and grateful for where God had brought me from in my life. I share this humorous story of my husband and I at the deli counter and my shouting for joy in the middle of the grocery store to emphasize that believers should always be grateful to God for what He has done in our lives.

No matter how large or small the victory, how silly or insignificant you may think it is, you should be grateful to God.

Living life with a grateful heart reveals your humility to God, acknowledging that you need Him to survive. Gratefulness provides the opportunity for the grace of God to work in your life. When you are grateful to God, you expand your capacity for increase and open the door for new opportunities from God. When God sees that you are overjoyed with the small things in life He will reward you with greater things in life. There is an old saying that says, "If you are not grateful for the lesser things in life, why would God give you greater?" So you must learn to be grateful for what you have and what God has done in your life because gratefulness let's God know how much you appreciate His loving kindness.

On the other hand, ungratefulness blocks the flow of God's blessings in your life and closes the door on new possibilities.

As you breathe God's Fresh Air, you should remain grateful for the good things that He has done in your life, *"giving thanks always for all things to God and the Father in the name of our Lord Jesus Christ"--Ephesians 5:20 (NLT)*. In other words, you should live life with a grateful heart and a thankful spirit. Appreciate the little things in life, be content with what you have, and do not take anything for granted. So I encourage you to be thankful to God for the things He has done and breathe God's Fresh Air with a grateful heart.

Chapter 10: Notes and Study Questions

Chapter Focus: *This chapter focuses on the importance of being thankful to God for the things that He has done in your life. The chapter encourages you to live life with a grateful heart which means you cherish the things that God has done and as a result you will begin to enjoy life more (Breathe God's Fresh Air).*

What good thing has God done in your life?

_____

_____

_____

_____

_____

_____

_____

_____

_____

What are you grateful for?

_____

_____

_____

_____

_____

_____

_____

_____

_____

_____

_____

_____

Alicia M. Bailey

Notes:

_____

_____

_____

_____

_____

_____

_____

_____

_____

_____

_____

_____

_____

_____

_____

_____

CHAPTER 11

THE CALL FOR SALVATION

After reading this book, if you desire to grow closer to the Lord or form a relationship with God through Jesus Christ then today is your day. Accepting Salvation is vital to Breathing Freely in the Lord. The Bible teaches that there is only one way to Heaven. Jesus said: "I am the way, the truth, and the life: no man cometh unto the Father but by me." (John 14:6)

<u>Accepting Salvation only requires a few things.</u>

1. **We must admit that we are sinners.** *"For all have sinned, and come short of the glory of God." --Romans 3:23(KJV)*
2. **Repent of our sin.** Jesus said: *"I tell you, Nay: but, except ye repent, ye shall all likewise perish."--Luke 13:5 (KJV)*
3. **Believe that Jesus Christ died for you, was buried, and rose from the dead.** *That if thou shalt confess with thy mouth the Lord Jesus, and shalt believe in thine heart that God hath raised Him from the dead, thou shalt be saved."--Romans 10:9 (KJV)*
4. **Pray the Prayer of Salvation; invite Jesus into your life to become your personal Savior.** *For with the heart man believeth unto righteousness; and with the mouth confession is made unto salvation."--Romans 10:10 (KJV)*

<u>Prayer of Salvation</u>

Dear God, I invite you into my heart. I repent of my sin and make you the Lord of my life. I believe that Jesus shed His blood, died for my sin, was buried, and rose from the dead. And now Holy Spirit come into my heart. I accept you into my life to lead me, guide me, teach me, and comfort me. As of this moment, I believe in my heart and confess with my mouth that I am saved. Thank-you Jesus for salvation and for your Holy Spirit within me. Amen!

After praying the Prayer of Salvation, be sure to visit the website at <u>www.aliciabaileyministries.com</u> for more information and remember to reach out to a Bible-based church in your area. Congratulations on your Salvation, welcome to the Body of Christ, and May God bless you on your spiritual journey.

THE END

ABOUT THE AUTHOR

Minister/Evangelist Alicia Bailey is the CEO/Founder of Alicia Bailey Ministries and Women Ministers Network Incorporated, a non-profit organization designed to empower and connect women preachers and ministers. With her inspirational vision and call to ministry, she has blessed the hearts of many through her preaching, teaching, and singing. Alicia Bailey is a native of Winston-Salem, North Carolina. She was born into a Christian family of many singers and ministers including, Gospel Legend Pastor Shirley Caesar.

Minister Bailey attended North Carolina Agricultural and Technical State University where she received her Bachelor of Science Degree in Education. She later attended Winston-Salem State University for graduate school where she received her Masters Degree in Education. Soon after, Minister Bailey attended Gardner Webb University where she earned her Principal and Administrative Licensure for Education. Minister Bailey has also studied Theology at Vintage Bible College.

God has called her as an evangelist to preach and spread the Gospel of Jesus Christ. Minister Bailey was called to minister and preached her initial sermon in 2006 under the leadership of the *Kimberly Park Holiness Church* where she first became the Youth Minister and later became an Associate Minister of the Ministry and Women's Ministry Coordinator. She was ordained and licensed for ministry under the doctrine of the *Holiness Church of God Inc.*, where Bishop Arnie Hunter Joyce is Presiding Senior Bishop. She currently serves under the spiritual guidance and in membership of *Love and Faith Christian Fellowship Church*, where Michael Thomas is Senior Pastor.

She has been blessed with a singing voice and talent. Minister Bailey began vocal training at the age of five. She joined the cast of the *National Black Repertory Company* in the production of "*The Black Nativity*" written by Langston Hughes. She has also appeared on the *"Praise Discovery Show"* in Atlanta, Georgia and was a finalist in the Ms. Gospel USA Pageant. She is also the author of the children's book *"RUNRU Kangaroo."*

Minister Bailey is the proud wife of Marquis Bailey of Winston-Salem, NC, who is an anointed man of God. Minister Bailey believes that God is calling for spiritual wholeness in men and women everywhere. She is determined to follow the Christian principles and teachings of the Lord Jesus Christ.

Printed in the United States
By Bookmasters